Prisms, Particles, and Refractions

poems by

Carol Smallwood

Finishing Line Press
Georgetown, Kentucky

Prisms, Particles, and Refractions

Copyright © 2017 Carol Smallwood
ISBN 978-1-63534-233-8 First Edition
All rights reserved under International and Pan-American Copyright Conventions. No part of this book may be reproduced in any manner whatsoever without written permission from the publisher, except in the case of brief quotations embodied in critical articles and reviews.

ACKNOWLEDGMENTS

Grateful acknowledgment to the publications in which the poems appeared:

Acoustic Ceilings and Tile Floors: *Intima: A Journal of Narrative Medicine,* Fall, 2015
The Beauty of Lace: *The Aurorean,* Winter 2004-2005; *Divining the Prime Meridian* (WordTech Editions, 2015)
The Blue of Swimming Pools: Linq December, 2011; *Water, Earth, Air, Fire, and Picket Fences* (Lamar University Press, 2014)
Chance: Crucible, 2011; *Compartments: Poems on Nature, Femininity and Other Realms* (Anaphora Literary Press, 2011)
Color of Water: *NEBO Literary Journal,* Spring 2017
A Dark Matter: *I-70 Review,* 2012
Dreams of Flying: *Compartments: Poems on Nature, Femininity and Other Realms* (Anaphora Literary Press, 2011)
First Snow: *Pennsylvania Literary Journal,* 2012
A Green So Emerald: *Third Wednesday,* Spring, 2011; *Compartments: Poems on Nature, Femininity and Other Realms* (Anaphora Literary Press, 2011)
The Hovering: *Parentheses Journal,* March 29, 2017; *Peacock Journal,* January 9, 2017
A Late Summer Diary: *Winter Tales II: Women on the Art of Aging* (Serving House Books, 2012)
On Days of Slow Rain: *Young Ravens Literary Review,* Issue 5, 2016
A Pastel Sestina: *Compartments: Poems on Nature, Femininity and Other Realms* (Anaphora Literary Press, 2011)
Photographs: *Contemporary American Voices,* July, 2014
The Pleiades: *The Society of Classical Poets,* 2016
A Prufrock Measurement: *Vox Poetica* July, 2012; *See Spot Run,* October, 2013
Sewing by Day: *Parentheses Journal,* March 29, 2017
Some Days: *Compartments: Poems on Nature, Femininity and Other Realms* (Anaphora Literary Press, 2011)
Strangest Thing of All: *Water, Earth, Air, Fire, and Picket Fences* (Lamar University Press, 2014)
A Tea Villanelle: *Compartments: Poems on Nature, Femininity and Other Realms* (Anaphora Literary Press, 2011)
There Were Only: *Heron Tree,* 2016
Trailing Wisps: *Transcendent Visions,* Fall 2004; *Water, Earth, Air, Fire, and Picket Fences* (Lamar University Press, 2014)
A Vision Triolet: The Yale Journal for Humanities in Medicine May 10, 2009; *Compartments: Poems on Nature, Femininity and Other Realms* (Anaphora Literary Press, 2011)
We See: *Water, Earth, Air, Fire, and Picket Fences* (Lamar University Press, 2014)

Publisher: Leah Maines
Editor: Christen Kincaid
Cover Art: Wikipedia
Author Photo: Cheboygan Daily Tribune
Cover Design: Elizabeth Maines McCleavy

Printed in the USA on acid-free paper.
Order online: www.finishinglinepress.com
    also available on amazon.com

Author inquiries and mail orders:
Finishing Line Press
P. O. Box 1626
Georgetown, Kentucky 40324
U. S. A.

Table of Contents

Contents

Foreword
Introduction

Prelude

To See Light

Prisms

Cuttlefish 1
Eclipses 2
A Tea Villanelle 3
Leaves Flourish in the Light 4
A Scattering of Lines 5
In the Dark 6
A Pastel Sestina Sans Meter 7
A Vision Triolet 9
Dreams of Flying 10
They Say 12
We See 13
Strangest Thing of All 14
The Beauty of Lace 15
Geography is 16
We Rejoice 17
Acoustic Ceilings and Tile Floors 18
Photographs 19
A Dark Matter 20
It Was a Great Privilege 21
First Snow 22
It Makes Life Possible 23
Trailing Wisps 24

Particles

A Cinquain to Progress 27
Against the Light 28
Beyond Known Laws 29
Live With It 30
Some Days 31
Three Dolls 32
Subterranean 33
The Third Floor 34
A Passing Sun 36
The Woman 37
You Know 38

Deep in Oceans...39
It is Agreed 40
Today There Came..41
In Analytical Logic Class...42
If..43
I Saw the First Hint 44
Two Dry Leaves 45
Signs 46
Lunch Time at Wendy's 47
The Blue of Swimming Pools 48
Points of the Compass 50

Refractions

On Days of Slow Rain 53
A Late Summer Diary 54
Water Puddles 58
Yes, I Will Stay..59
The Sun Acquires 60
Plants..61
Sewing by Day..62
The Train Whistled..63
There Were Only..64
Today the Car...65
This Morning 66
Icons..67
Sleep is Wasted...68
With Eyes Wide Open 69
A Beginning...70
A Fun Jumble 71
When Young...72
Solar Eclipses...73
A Prufrock Measurement..74
The Pleiades...75
Chameleon Light 76
There Are Many...77
Arranging Spices on Your Shelf 78
A Spider..79
Color of Water 80
On Hot Summer Days 81
It's Immaterial..82

Epilogue

A Green So Emerald

Foreword

Long before I was an editor of *Contemporary American Voices*, I was a poet. And long before that I was a voracious reader of poetry. As a poet, I have learned that submitted work is often a matter of taste, a particular feeling, light in an editor's mind. For years, prior to being an editor, I have been a fan of Carol Smallwood. Not only does her poetry resonate in a reader's heart and mind, it encapsulates a mood. It sets a tone and challenges you to recognize "the beauty of lace". In the July 2014 issue of *Contemporary American Voices,* Carol Smallwood was the Featured Poet, with five short pieces of tuned-in work. What is so extraordinary about Prisms, Particles, and Refractions is its vision and identification of darkness. An absolutely stunning collection worthy of a thorough read or two or three. A book, once bought, has found its forever home.

Lisa Zaran, founder and editor of *Contemporary American Voices*

Introduction

Light has been studied since ancient times to contemporary quantum mechanics—we know that nothing travels faster. It is something we take for granted but once we begin to try and understand light, find it has many mysteries yet hidden.

Prisms, Particles, and Refractions is a collection of free verse and formal poems all poems aimed at capturing some of the aspects of light—light that our eyes detect and light also as metaphor. Most of the poems are serious but some have a pinch of humor found to help perspective.

The seventy-three poems are divided into: Prelude; Prisms; Particles; Refractions; Epilogue. It is hoped the poems bring as much enjoyment to readers as they did in the writing. My sincere thanks to poet and editor, Lisa Zaran for writing the foreword, Carole Mertz for proofreading, and Jeffrey Makala, Chris Swanberg, Mary Barnet, Katherine Mayfield, Sarah Cisse for the blurbs.

Carol Smallwood

Prelude

To See Light

one must first have eyes that can see—
but it isn't that simple. Light has properties
of both waves and particles that move
in wave-like patterns best understood
by quantum mechanics.

Prisms

Cuttlefish

survive by matching their
environment, changing the
color and texture of skin
in a blink of W-shaped
pupil eyes; they dazzle
with light patterns like
some marquee—if that
doesn't work, they exit
in an inky cloud

Eclipses

If you stay in a certain place,
you may see partial eclipses—
but for a total eclipse,
you must travel to where
day becomes night.

A Tea Villanelle

Once the lid's off you see bubbles align
On the Wendy's cup like Braille,
The hot water dots shape no evident design

I lift the styrofoam cup like mulled wine
Or in adoration of the Holy Grail—
Once the lid's off you see bubbles align

Copernicus didn't change how the sun shines
Even when his theory wasn't thought a tale:
The hot water dots shape no evident design

I pull apart the tea bag looking for a sign
But the string-joined bag leaves no trail,
The hot water dots shape no evident design

The bubbles pop after their water climb
Or hug the edges as if impaled
While the tea darkens with time

Raising my cup I toast customers in line
Hoping their quests do not fail;
Once the lid's off you see bubbles align,
The hot water dots shape no evident design

Leaves Flourish in the Light

Solanum tuberosum has been domesticated a lot of years:
from the U.S. to Chile their leaves flourish in the light.
Potatoes aren't visible until dug with some cheers,
washed, dried, sorted—harvested in plain sight.

From the U.S. to Chile their leaves flourish in the light:
selective breeding assures mashed, hashed, boiled, fried—
washed, dried, sorted—harvested in plain sight.
the ways to prepare them are numerous, very wide.

Selective breeding assures mashed, hashed, boiled, fried;
the vegetable, vulnerable to molds, doesn't keep as well as grain.
The ways to prepare them are numerous, very wide;
letting them rot on shelves is deserving of shame.

The vegetable, vulnerable to molds, doesn't keep as well as grain.
Potatoes aren't visible until dug with some cheers—
letting them rot on the shelf is deserving of shame:
Solanum tuberosum has been domesticated a lot of years.

A Scattering of Lines

Sunlight would reach Earth in a straight line
if it weren't for the layer of air—
light traveling in a straight line by design.
Sunlight would reach Earth in a straight line
but is scattered by air molecules with such flare
it makes the blue sky daily fare.
Sunlight would reach Earth in a straight line
if it weren't for the layer of air.

In the Dark

The power went out after rising from a chair;
there was no wind, rain, snow so why did it go out?
Being in the dark is uncomfortable to bear
so felt my way for a flashlight to get about.

There was no wind, rain, snow so why did it go out?
I called the power company but was given no hope
so felt my way for a flashlight to get about:
I'd had to wait like this before and wouldn't mope.

I called the power company but was given no hope.
The silence closed as if in a grave;
I'd had to wait like this before and wouldn't mope
and whistled loudly to seem brave.

The silence closed as if in a grave
as my flashlight caught the swirling dust
and whistled loudly to seem brave;
I began sewing by guess to feel less nonplussed

as my flashlight caught the swirling dust.
Being in the dark is uncomfortable to bear;
I began sewing by guess to feel less nonplussed—
the power went out after rising from a chair.

A Pastel Sestina Sans Meter

I called the Avon Lady to help me feel more at home
and looked forward to a possible way to meet others.
"Do you know you have a wasp's nest by your door?"
"Oh, is that right?" I asked trying to sound concerned.
The Avon lady extended a calendar saying, "I know it's
late for a calendar but aren't the colors so pastel?"

To my nod, she added, "The pictures have such fresh pastel
appeal don't they? You know, I don't have the breeze at home
that you do here," I saw her nose carefully detecting its
scent—my neighbor's dairy herd. She sat not as others,
back not touching the couch figuring me out, concerned
where I fit in the scheme while glaring at my screen door.

"My grandchildren are husky boys that knock on my door
asking for my baked cookies but wish I could buy pastel
dresses for girls." I looked at her catalog concerned
with remembering, bringing back love: "You rush home
to greet him with laughter and love," girls and others
dipping hands in a dappled stream smiling like it's

always spring. I see slim models making me believe it's
the only way women should be, children going out the door
with baskets of strawberries. Rose petals and others
graced pages that matched the lipstick, a pale pastel
called Eternal Blush, worn by the Avon Lady. Her home
I imagined as pale, matching; she was concerned

that I would get the next catalog out, quite concerned
if I wasn't home she'd give the bag an extra twist so it's
sure wind wouldn't carry it off. Avon gives a sense of home,
of belonging as American as the *Reader's Digest*. My door
knob would hang the next catalog. Did filters make the pastel
shades misty vanishing outlines for creams, and others?

Even lotion (pour le corps) had pastel labels, others
too, but saw that catalogs were also now concerned

with cell phones. She confided, "Women like to use pastel
so much. It's so delightful, so feminine, romantic, it's
so flattering, comforting, my dear," going out the door;
I'd hang the calendar she'd extended on a wall in my home.

I'd look forward to the next catalog from the Avon Lady,
will watch my front and side door with a concerned look,
guessing next year's calendar will also be pastel.

A Vision Triolet

A digital fundus photo is quick,
recommended for anyone just in case—
each eye must stare till photographic;
a digital fundus photo is quick,
the results rival a *National Geographic*
glossy spectacular of outer space.
The digital fundus photo is quick
recommended for anyone just in case.

The optometrist pointed to murky stains
"Due to common aging," he explained
fed by vessels deep in my brain.
The optometrist pointed to murky stains
foreign as a NASA Mars terrain—
the exposure, dull red, self-contained.
The optometrist pointed to murky stains
"due to common aging," he explained.

Dreams of Flying

"You know, when I come back to River City, I turn
into what I once was," said Karen. I hadn't seen her
since our last school reunion and her eyes looked
blurred—it could be contacts. I'd stayed in
River City known for the world's largest man-made
sand pile from dredging in lumbering days,

which sat like a pyramid on the Nile; on days
of high wind when it wasn't wet or weather had a turn
of snow, it made eyes smart. Perhaps a man-made
answer explained Karen's blurred look. She waved her
hand with many rings saying her husband had left in
a hurry with a woman who sold tennis balls, then looked

out the window saying, "I loved him but looked
like I didn't like him and I've spent so many long days
crying," then showed me pictures of her poodles. In
time the talk was about classmates, and in turn
I asked if she liked the service. She'd done well, her
rise was rapid and she'd been able to buy man-made

goods I could never have. Twisting a man-made
heart shaped ring she waited a minute, and then looked
at me to ask, "What's your idea of Heaven?, her
tone returning to the best friend of high school days.
She continued, "I've been having these dreams. I turn
and twist among dark blue clouds looking down in

flight seeing days go by, listening, everything in
plain sight, not afraid of falling or landing in man-made
or natural places and easily fly, effortlessly turn
to gulp fresh air, satisfying a deep thirst it looked
I never had. When I awake I feel cast out for days."
We talked about River City and I poured her

more coffee and after salad the talk changed to her
aunt she was visiting. I just couldn't forget that in

high school she dropped me, joined the in crowd only days
into our junior year. My husband had left no man-made
things when he left in a hurry: hard as I tried it looked
like I had little to give her than lunch in turn.

Not many days after I heard Karen was dead. I saw her
turn and say, "looked like I didn't like him" recalled
her list of man-made things, dropping me in high school.

They Say

seeing is believing but during any day
who can believe the world's round,
with no natural light without the sun?

That the clouds are a very thin layer—
beyond is incomprehensible black space?

That our planet is just one of many—
that black holes consume everything?

And yet, who has seen the wind?

We See

with rods and cones I learned
in college—it may not be true
today

The first mirrors must've been
bodies of water, faces
surfaces that reflect

Who was the first to make a mirror?
Were they sacrificed to the gods?

But we still see upside down:
images adjusted automatically
as in caveman days

Strangest Thing of All

When Lily turned on the bathroom light she recalled her
psychology professor stressing the importance of
asking questions.

In philosophy, her professor admired Bertrand Russell;
but was Russell just a way not to not believe in anything,
that drifting, formless bed of marshmallows,
the misery of *Inferno's* first circle?

While Cal snored, she concluded the strangest thing
of all was not to see how strange things were.

The Beauty of Lace

lies in what is missing
as much as in what is there—
in repetition, regular
form, revealing the
underneath

I suspect atoms are not
dissimilar.

Geography is

North

Stone comes from the core
of the earth. Michelangelo
knew the Carrara quarry of
Roman times and "David"
stands that way because the
stone was flawed. My core
is stone too large to move
in my grandfather's field

South

Trees in White Rapids don't
grow very tall—wet ground
not supporting them. They
grow in clumps and when
reaching too high, topple
together

East

October sky is a mosaic
of refracted sun lacking
definition or depth, a gold
hurrah for dreamers:
a hazy harbinger of winter
when gold-colored glasses
are worn by fools

West

Sand forms when rock breaks,
and, carried by wind, water,
or ice, often finds water:
if buried deep enough, long
enough, returns to rock

We Rejoice

seeing the first green weed
moved by its brave emergence
in brown landscape.

Bold, slim, solitary,
the weed lords it over life
yet untrusting of spring.

Acoustic Ceilings and Tile Floors

Doctor visits are lying on tables looking at ceiling tiles,
looking down on tile floors while weighed on scales
all the time thinking you'd like to be visiting the British Isles,
picturing extravagant meals in the garden of Versailles.

Looking down on tile floors while weighed on scales
you count the white flecks in one of the beige squares
picturing extravagant meals in the garden of Versailles
and what life must be like for a charge d'affaires.

You count the white flecks in one of the beige squares;
do you have time to count them all—
and what life must be like for a charge d'affaires
to not wonder what made a dent in the white wall.

Do you have time to count them all
while not looking at the long scissors on tables?
To not wonder what made a dent in the white wall
you try to guess how many others thought of fables.

While not looking at the long scissors on tables
waiting for the doctor to walk through the door
you try to guess how many others thought of fables,
any other thing to take you away, make you soar

waiting for the doctor to walk through the door.
All the time thinking you'd like to be visiting the British Isles,
any other thing to take you away, make you soar.
Doctor visits are lying on tables looking at ceiling tiles.

Photographs

of Earth reveal a
naked blue marble
with cloud wisps.

I make Florida orange,
Japan purple like my
childhood globe secured
by longitude and latitude.

A Dark Matter

Observers learned by watching rotation
that galaxies are nearly 90% invisible dark matter
which confounds our very best contemplation.
Observers learned by watching rotation
that without dark matter galaxies lack consolidation
and would collapse in one cosmic splatter.
Observers learned by watching rotation
that galaxies are nearly 90% invisible dark matter.

It Was a Great Privilege

to be there in the club chair in the library: only the affluent
once could read. And today was special because a good
night's sleep was recompense for nights counting oars
in the River Styx.

Recompense too for waiting for needed rain. For getting
all the flies from between the windows in the dining room
by putting a container over them, pushing a paper underneath
and carrying them outside.

Back and forth, back and forth. It seemed like I got them
all and others appeared. How did they get there anyway?

Kitty came to look but returned to washing her paws
in a sunbeam on the floor.

First Snow

First snow of the season should be
viewed as a child sees: the strangeness,
the whimsical, democratic oddity
that's snow

Still, children do not see it
as water transubstantiation or
as the color virgins wore when
sacrificed to the gods

Today it came, slow, lopsided
dots if learning, only to change
on some command to fine,
slanting lines

Sometimes it descends—a flurry of
rice tossed at weddings quickly
melted, making you doubt it ever
was

It Makes Life Possible

The Greeks called it Helios, the Egyptians Ra, we call it Sun:
it makes life possible but if it comes too close it'll destroy us;
it could hold a million earths this esteemed number one.
The Greeks called it Helios, the Egyptians Ra, we call it Sun:
if it burned out we wouldn't know till 8 minutes after it was done
and would end things—the last fatal digress.
The Greeks called it Helios, the Egyptians Ra, we call it Sun:
it makes life possible but if it comes too close it'll destroy us.

Trailing Wisps

Hearing a distant
Train and picturing
Trailing wisps of white,
I realized with
Surprise that trains
Hadn't smoked for
Years; that
Conjured grace of
Trailing wisps had
Been illusions—and
Smoke wouldn't
Been white.

The whistle
Became reedy
Disjointed threads
The closer the train
Came. When it left
Quavering, as if
Entangled in the wind,
I turned into a wisp
Of white and trailed
It out of town.

Particles

A Cinquain to Progress

Helios in Greek myth traveled by chariot as a Sun god
with what Pindar describes "fire-darting steeds" each day
across the sky. The horses with fiery manes flying roughshod
bore such names as Pyrois, Phlegon, ignored earthly sod
and faithfully make daily trips without delay.

The Sun, the center of our Solar System, our source
of all life and energy has a core that produces most
of its energy through nuclear fusion with efficient force
changing hydrogen into helium. It disperses a lethal dose
that—if not for the Earth's magnetic field we'd roast.

Knowledge pushes on: NASA has plans for a mission
to measure particles and energy coming from the Sun
another on how it creates and controls its own heliosphere.
Einstein's simple equation on energy however austere
preceded the atomic bomb: progress stole a home run.

Against the Light

Watermarks are visible when held against light
whispering quality, distinction, louder than a shout—
are also used in banknotes ensuring they're alright:
some marks are more visible than others that are about.

Whispering quality, distinction, louder than a shout
made by subtle paper thickness and density variations
some marks are more visible than others that are about
in passports, stamps, and other applications.

Made by subtle paper thickness and density variations
watermarks can show quality, mill trademarks, age
in passports, stamps, and other applications
providing a crucial consumer protection gauge.

Watermarks can show quality, mill trademarks, age
are also used in banknotes ensuring they're alright
providing a crucial consumer protection gauge:
Watermarks are visible when held against light.

Beyond Known Laws

Black holes are discovered by reactions of what they near—
the event horizon of black holes is called Point of No Return.
Black holes emit no light and are without peers:
whatever enters has no hope of escape or making kick turns.

The event horizon of black holes is called Point of No Return:
at the heart of our galaxy is one 15 million miles across—
whatever enters has no hope of escape or making kick turns:
a possible gate to space itself—more than just scientific gloss.

At the heart of our galaxy is one 15 million miles across,
the core of an exploded super nova (an extra large star)
a possible gate to space itself—more than just scientific gloss:
they're unfathomable, beyond known laws, completely bizarre.

The core of an exploded super nova (an extra large star),
black holes emit no light and are without peers—
they're unfathomable, beyond known laws, completely bizarre.
Black holes are discovered by reactions of what they near.

Live With It

There wasn't a warning, just jagged lightning in one eye
then a film with bits and tatters of detached floating black.
When the doctor said cataract surgery wouldn't help, I sighed.

He joked: "It's your meanness coming out in this hot July
and you could try moving them by becoming a jumping jack;"
There wasn't a warning, just jagged lightning in one eye.

He added, "Maybe a pogo stick would make them go awry"
but all I could picture was falling and needing an ice pack.
When the doctor said cataract surgery wouldn't help, I sighed.

A few years ago I'd been told to buy a leutein supply
for macular degeneration due to aging—there was no going back;
there wasn't a warning, just jagged lightning in one eye.

The doctor said to live with it and get used to the black flies
but it is hard to acquire that particular coping knack:
when the doctor said cataract surgery wouldn't help, I sighed.

I'm grateful surgery isn't needed as the days go by
but wish the vision I had before would just come back.
There wasn't a warning, just jagged lightning in one eye.
When the doctor said cataract surgery wouldn't help, I sighed.

Some Days

In the spring when pushing a cart down aisles she
wore a tiara of seed pearls and in the fall, rubies.
Some days trains were of ermine, other days crackling
taffeta; her diamonds the size of robin eggs on both
hands and the size of lima beans as buttons; samples
extended in paper cups were not Wisconsin cider
but French champagne in long stem crystal handed
out not by gum chewing Babs or Trudi in uniforms
with slips showing, but ladies in flowing velvet.
She imagined what they (her subjects) were saying
about her beauty and clothes, how they'd die for her.
Tears filled her eyes seeing her funeral procession
with grief stricken subjects tossing rose petals.

Three Dolls

Three dolls who've survived the years are together in one place
 grouped out of direct light as if enjoying tea and conversation
 as they sit in pink dresses showing cracked faces with grace.

Time and changing circumstances cannot erase
 the security of keeping them in full view, a compensation:
 three dolls who've survived the years are together in one place.

Their dresses are mostly in good repair despite torn lace
 but wish I could hear what they talked about—a translation
 as they sit in pink dresses showing cracked faces with grace.

I have them under a table so they don't take up much space
 and wonder if their end may also be cremation:
 three dolls who've survived the years are together in one place.

They've been around so long I touch base
 with them to help aging trepidation
 as they sit in pink dresses showing cracked faces with grace.

I've thought of sending them away to restore their faces
 but if lost there wouldn't be any possible replication:
 three dolls who've survived the years are together in one place
 as they sit in pink dresses showing cracked faces with grace.

Subterranean

It's chilling to view pictures of our blue planet in space:
science says molten red rock churns under our feet—
shifting tectonic plates must be accepted with grace:
worry is useless—there's no such thing as retreat.

Science says molten red rock churns under our feet—
landslides, volcanoes, earthquakes, tsunami, come every year;
worry is useless—there's no such thing as retreat—
that continents constantly shift causes insecurity and fear.

Landslides, volcanoes, earthquakes, tsunami, come every year.
Magma (like our subconscious) is unseen:
that continents constantly shift causes insecurity and fear,
encouraging wonder what it's about, what it could mean.

Magma (like our subconscious) is unseen:
shifting tectonic plates must be accepted with grace
encouraging wonder what it's about, what it could mean.
It's chilling to view pictures of our blue planet in space.

The Third Floor

1

I was in the library reading a review of Czeslaw Milosz: how he
saw language as failing to capture ontological reality. Trying to
figure what it meant, I noticed the wind must've risen from the
moving branches. The branches curved inward and there was
a scar on the trunk where a branch had been. The tree was
too far away to identify its leaves but it was next to a blue spruce
unresponsive to wind. Each gust made the leaves move differently.
You could gauge the wind more clearly by using the window frame
like a T-square. Did the wind make the clouds move or is it
because the earth spins? Clouds over a utility pole topped it
like Cool Whip. When leaving, coffee drifted from the lobby café
congenial as a handshake. Once again I tried to appreciate an
untitled piece at the foot of the stairs made of parts from a defunct
Great Lakes Tool & Die. It'd started to rain—or could it be snow?
But it was too early for snow; still, it drifted like snow and was
white like snow.

2

The next day I sat at a study carrel one back from the previous day
so the view was different. The day was much brighter and not as
windy so I lined up with narrowed eyes the clouds on the windowsill
which were rounded on top like ads for baking powder biscuits.
I framed part of the sky with trees on the left and my shoulder on
the right using the window as the top and bottom. Turning my head
upside down made it all new till alternating blasts of a siren
(installed after 9/11) surprised me. I read a study about computers
as the fundamental mechanisms of thought but kept nodding off.
After a critique on a biography of Linus Pauling, a chemist who did
his best work outside a laboratory, the light from the window began
to fade and it was time to join the pedestrians below who looked
so small.

3

The third day was cloudless. The window was filled with reflections of fluorescent lights—rows and rows of them which, when lined up, were planes on a runway. There were two flies but they were outside and were free. There were fewer leaves.

A Passing Sun

Spring winds bring smiles to those who see
coyly revealed underside of leaves
before blossoms come for honey bees

It's all too easy in September to believe
the winds of spring were just imagination
a passing sun conceived

and relegate spring to a brief flirtation—
a flitting grace note in one's vacation

The Woman

slumped in a chemo chair watched
TV with flushed face and open mouth.

She wore velcro shoes, a yellow
t-shirt with bumblebees.

I noticed her because she never moved
and her logo was: "Busy as a Bee."

You Know

it's Truth when it's
simple, elegant,
somehow familiar—
leaving you washed
in disbelief you never
saw it before.

Deep in Oceans

too far for light, species generate
their own light, a process called
bioluminescence.

It is also useful out of water:
fireflies use it to locate mates.

It is Agreed

we must see before know but—
the universe is mostly unknown
dark energy and dark matter.

Today There Came

a PIZZA & PLANNING postcard from Dent Family Funeral Chapel:
a number to reserve free pizza, information about preplanning funerals—
memorial questions would be answered.

I pictured myself eating hot pepperoni pizza with lots of cheese;
the boxes of pop-up tissues, thick flowered carpeting.
Pictures with fluffy clouds, light filtered by stained glass.

The glossy card was scattered with green leaves destined to be
recycled like ashes in my will—I'd eased the burden of dying,
like the postcard said.

In Analytical Logic Class

we're on the picture theory of language:

a proposition (picture of reality)
is a picture and to understand a
proposition is to understand what
it pictures.

What could Wittgenstein have
been seeing?

If

light falls in a forest and no one
is around to see it, is it visible?

I Saw the First Hint

of light come cocooned
in a white sheet winding
night and day

Two Dry Leaves

remained
in gray October
quivering
on the
tree—
tassels
of an aging
burlesque queen.

Signs

Signs in White Rapids are either small, nonexistent, or faded.
Even the hospital has a barely noticeable sign like if you didn't
know where it was you had no business going.

When old cartographers drew maps having unknown areas,
they named them Unknown Terrors, Ultima Thule,
with fanciful illustrations of mythical creatures.

When I went to the bank, I caught snatches on the red digital
newsline: Pittsburg Pirates 9 saves/opposing peace
with Palestine/bases loaded in the ninth/killing of
Saddam Hussein's sons/your bank has the best mortgage rates.

When waiting at a stop light, a NPR announcer said that most
musicals so popular during the Great Depression were lavish
escapist productions because people didn't want to see what
was going on. The stop light, one of those with green flashing
arrows for turns, seemed a square dance caller guiding cars to
take an Allemande Left or an Allemande Right on their
promenade home. Do Sa Do Around the Left-Hand Lady....

Stop lights in Nicolet City didn't have those flashing green
arrows. I remember one snowy Christmas Eve coming home
with the kids after Midnight Mass waiting for the one stop light
in Nicolet City. The kids had laughed because we hadn't seen
a car for miles; the red was the only color in our trip.

Lunch Time at Wendy's

People wandered by not unlike the *Canterbury Tales* while the
Beatles belted out, *I Want to Hold Your Hand*; people so alike
and so unalike, so endlessly interesting. A customer didn't go
through the maze of railings but went directly to the counter.
Then another did the same and others just kept falling in behind.

A woman walked in. Her handbag (the kind Queen Elizabeth carried)
was extended over her wrist as she made her way to the counter in
sensible shoes. She took a long time counting her money and the
cashier cupped her mouth to hide a grin.

I kept straining to see some detail in customers to define myself
and once again wondered how people could become science fiction
addicts when what's real is so fantastic.

The natives of Alaska had so many names for snow because
they observed their world; I'd lived long enough in Nicolet City
to know that the different sounds of waves were more than
I'd ever guess.

In White Rapids, ordering the same thing was not unlike the
variations of a theme: no two baked potatoes were the same.

Where could I go after? Not where I'd see tabloid headlines such as:
"3500-Year-Old Mummy Gives Birth"
"Oprah Loses 63 Pounds to Marry Elvis."

The place mat showed a portion of a Big Bacon Classic Cheeseburger
under a magnifying glass with a slice of red tomato kissed by
condensation, lettuce, bacon, cheese, and hamburger.

When I walked to my car, a man motioned me to walk by,
lowered the window of his pick-up, grinned, adjusted his baseball cap
to say, "I believe in beauty before age."

The Blue of Swimming Pools

With power out—people were stocking water and ice:
I thought it wise to drive to town.
The stoplights weren't working but people were polite,
it looked the same; the only grocery open was Brown's.

I thought it wise to drive to town.
People were pushing carts, nothing was different,
it looked the same—the only grocery open was Brown's;
the store had power but customers looked indifferent

people were pushing carts, nothing was different.
I checked on ice, thoroughly enjoying the cool air.
The store had power but customers looked indifferent;
it was good to be out and it was hard not to stare.

I checked on ice, thoroughly enjoying the cool air
stocking things that didn't require refrigeration.
It was good to be out and it was hard not to stare,
not to laugh at the tabloid photo of alien navigation,

buying things that didn't require refrigeration.
The small alien carrying a limp woman made it impossible
not to laugh at the tabloid photo of alien navigation.
The bags of ice were colder than I thought possible;

the small alien carrying a limp woman made it impossible,
quite beyond belief. The letters on the ice were blue,
the bags of ice were colder than I thought possible;
the fleeting pleasures of hot days can be very few.

Quite beyond belief, the letters on the ice were blue
soothing, the blue of swimming pools, hills of snow,
the fleeting pleasures of hot days can be very few.
With lots of water and ice I leave Brown's in the know:

soothing, the blue of swimming pools, hills of snow.
The stoplights weren't working but people were polite,

with lots of water and ice I leave Brown's in the know
with power out—people were stocking water and ice.

Points of the Compass

Solitary in soliloquy,
trees stand in a
game of Statues—
where flung, they stay

After a doctor's diagnosis
you see the other side of
the Moon and know underfoot
is molten lava

Today a professor neither young
nor old pronounced, "Men and
women are pretty much the same"

It sounded so democratic/equal
opportunity—and he had a
doctorate

Yet I wanted to say:
"No, we're from completely
different galaxies not
from Venus and Mars"

Every spring flowers bloom and
their fragrant beauty makes us
forget their purpose:
reproduction

Refractions

On Days of Slow Rain

I'm a child again
longing to read
darkened tree bark
like Braille

A Late Summer Diary

Wanting off the merry-go-round, I trudge the library stairs to the 4th floor to capture the subterranean to clarify what is called real. It was summer so not many were around to interrupt the basking of books, the labels neatly marching shelf after shelf—a glorious movable feast.

The bookshelves have signs to guide, buttons to move the phalanx, every third shelf with a light like a helmet. I breathe deeply the cool air to capture the illusive scent when banished and homesick for it, wishing to be part of it like the incense of childhood Mass.

There was a moth on the carpet and slipped it in a container carried in my purse for such rescues. There were no windows that opened so how did it get there? When driving in, I'd lined my tires so I'd run over a possum killed on the road to be sure it was killed and wondered again why wings of smashed birds move as if trying to fly.

When I put the moth on some Queen Anne's Lace at home it didn't move. I carried it to my plants, sprinkled it with water; at least the moth was now on soil—I wouldn't look tomorrow and believe it'd flown away as there were still some summer days ahead.

Day 2

The label from some shirt is still on the sidewalk as I walk to the library. There is a breeze for which I am grateful.

The 3rd floor reading room seemed waiting; the scent wasn't that of books though and the lack of high shelving like the 4th floor made the air flow more, a coolness almost too cool. A couple by the window: young, the guy's head in headscarf, a cough from someone unseen.

The Times Literary Supplement had Sanskrit books on the back cover. To know there were such sets was reassuring even though it prompted how little I knew about life that old; to review such a world must be a rare privilege and yet 3,000 years is the width of an eyelash.

To see the earth as an ever-expanding universe turns everything irrelevant so it is best to believe the earth is the center of the universe. Women are closer to the way things are but with this reality comes a greater need for illusions.

Day 3

Websites are jotted down surreptitiously as if fearing disapproval from peering books, stuffed in my purse.

Last night a DVD on the Tower of London showed a ceremony of locking doors performed ever since a king entered unchallenged on his return to England. The door ceremony is observed even on Christmas and continued during the Blitz: it is reassuring to think that since the 1300s the ceremony is performed every night at the same time and place.

Hope Kitty doesn't have another fur ball because it's hard leaving her at the vet's. My first decision after hearing I had cancer was putting her to sleep before I went and she changed then too, lost a lot of her bravado and started sitting by the house at dusk just staring west.

Heard from a Holocaust survivor. On one hand I envy her because her loss is clear, her pain a known cause. The Holocaust, like child and marital abuse are still being denied. She could be a relative and I'd never know because none of mine would admit anything.

It is good to be at Wendy's. I go to the post office to join the throng, the business people opening the larger boxes carrying cell phones swooping in and out with little ceremony.

Another Day

Am writing while eating at Wendy's. One must eat every day but libraries should be kept in awe, special places of last resort—I've learned that it is wise, necessary, to keep what you value most at bay to dole out.

Scheduled fall class, switching an unknown lady professor for a man one. He is good and didn't want to chance the unknown and it's nice to see a male, a thinking male, 3 times a week. So much for supporting my own sex. The class is fantasy and science fiction which I've avoided, bent on truth finding—wisdom does not come with age and yet a part of me won't admit it.

I'm the only one here feasting at Wendy's except for the employees who extend good-humored smiles to a regular. Kitty didn't stay out long this morning because it was too windy. I brush her often every day till she scratches.

That front part of my house under the picture window is a problem—gravel when I moved but when weeds came I hadn't the desire to destroy them. I put in more stones and weeds still came. I took the stones out and put Snow on the Mountain to take over.

Weeds still came. The lawn man sprayed to no avail and won't call him back because wild lilies have come to join Queen Anne's Lace.

September 2

It is the day before Labor Day. Time to drink my coffee instead of taking it home like spoils of war—not many around—students have gone home for the long weekend. The coffee is very good after a night of trying to sleep.

My writing is jagged because of the grains of sugar on the table—the end of the coffee is the best because sugar settles there.

Good to feel the pen when so much time is on computer keys: a pen somehow makes one feel more in control, like breadcrumbs for Hansel and Gretel.

Hospital floors come to mind with dots one follows gratefully because all the halls and doors look the same. Those polished floors, square tiles, beige, some set diagonal for style. Wish I could find that quote about style being shaped by limitation—best not to remember the whole file wiped out trying to change one quote.

Another hot flash from post-chemo pills. I wonder what hall my uterus traveled for disposal and imagine a long line of red circus dots. The surgeon in scrubs had been nibbling fruitcake when I was wheeled in the day before Christmas. The next day my tray had an evergreen sprig tied in red which I threw across the room—the aide called it a hormone thing.

My breasts were removed at another hospital but the floors were still beige and the white sheets also spotted with red.

We should dwell in the moment but only children can. And in diaries one does not have to apologize.

Water Puddles

reflect skies with such
clarity I'm a child again,
staring at trees upside
down till tipsy—
not remembering
underfoot lava flows
rivaling the heat
of the Sun

Yes, I Will Stay

a bit longer at Wendy's—
the sun has crept beyond
the partition and I don't
often linger

Turning eyes sideway, I see
six suns in a row swirling on
the rim of my glasses

The words I write on a slant
fade like the Cheshire Cat
as conversations pass

Returning to the first home
solely mine, the sun flickers
through trees, a fractured cinema

The Sun Acquires

a brave dimension in November
battling clouds to warm shorn fields,
granting light to those who seek it.

Plants

by the roadsides, ditches, railroad tracks
are among the last of their species.

In plain sight they survive because they're
invisible.

Sewing by Day

A chair by a window is best for selecting pieces in quilt making:
light of day, natural light, best reveals shades, flaws in pieces
of boxes on boxes of clothes carefully cut—a slow undertaking;
quilt after quilt has made my children question output increases.

Light of day, natural light, best reveals shades, flaws in pieces.
"Who's your quilts for?" I'm asked as stacked quilts grow higher.
Quilt after quilt has made my children question output increases
and I picture the stacks after I'm gone going up in a night pyre.

"Who's your quilts for?" I'm asked as stacked quilts grow higher:
plaid, plain, striped, flowered, flannel, fleece, denim, cotton
and I picture the stacks after I'm gone going up in a night pyre—
memories stored in cut clothes and pieces not yet forgotten.

Plaid, plain, striped, flowered, flannel, fleece, denim, cotton
of boxes on boxes of clothes carefully cut—a slow undertaking:
memories stored in cut clothes and pieces not yet forgotten.
A chair by a window is best for selecting pieces in quilt making.

The Train Whistled

when I was in the bank looking at *Newsweek* covers
waiting for my sorted coins for the humane society
to be counted:

March 10 was on how faith shaped President Bush's
life and presidency;
March 17 was on biological weapons and urban warfare;
March 24 was about why America scares the world with
a picture of MOAB (Mother Of All Bombs);
March 31 was on "Shock and Awe," Baghdad on fire.

The bank had Support Our Troops U.S. flag posters for
sale with yellow ribbons on lampposts and tree trunks.

When the train whistled again I wondered what direction
it was going.

There Were Only

a few lights on in the library, no car tracks in the parking lot,
a gentle rain reinforcing the nose as the most elemental of
the senses. It was a much-needed rain that could be too late
for crops—a neighbor saying corn ears were very small.
So much rain early spring and then the lushness turns brittle
brown.

Maybe there weren't any car tracks in the parking lot because
of the rain but when I reached the library, a couple said it was
closed. It was sad to think of computers blinking in the empty
library like solitary lighthouses.

I lift my face to capture the rain of childhood and failing,
remember the earth is covered mostly with water and we
know less about oceans than the moon. So many wonders
lost in grade school.

Today the Car

ahead had a sticker: As Real As It Gets. It was windy—
bags and flyers scurrying the street.

When I got in the lab room, the chair had the same hospital
auxiliary bluebird pillow, employees the same photo badge
stars and strips. The aide abandoned my arm for my hand
and didn't respond to my question, "How much do you need?"
so watched the wall clock and wondered why magazines
featured makeup to make you look natural.

The car wash had a grinning boy with muffled ears who
emerged in the mist waving white towels in a jet roar.
After reaching *Put Car in Drive When You See This Sign*
I followed the tracks of those before.

Driving home, the tips of corn that'd emerged in spring
in such straight lines had become cracking gold—
in July their uniforms sinuous emerald.

This Morning

there appeared to be a stick on my door but
not trusting appearances, I got a paper to lift it
off and the six inches moved—yes it was one
of those six-legged walking stick bugs with legs
arched as if on a motorcycle. I moved it to the
grass then returned and brought it in to look at
with a magnifying glass. Kitty watched.

It had bamboo brown segments and legs that
branched off from brown were pine needle green.
It also had the same green in 2 long feelers
coming from its head that in repose, were
folded hands. It moved slowly, feeling its way
with front legs although under the magnifying
glass I could see eyes on each side of a head that
seemed but the end of its brown stick body.
Its tail a loop like a needle eye.

We watched each other till I put it in the
woods on a fallen tree.

Icons

After watching a program on the Sphinx,
my cat with outstretched paws seemed
to copy its mystery.

Theories abound about the Sphinx—
as many questions as the *Mona Lisa*.

The more icons are studied in plain sight
the less (like cats) we understand.

Sleep is Wasted

on the young—their slates too clean,
no burs stick in ragged corners.

The rest of us walk with sacks of
flour dreaming of ballet.

With Eyes Wide Open

Visuals were on a screen in the waiting room:
I watched since I couldn't manage print to read
waiting for the yearly eye exam to resume
as dilation time ran on its own slow speed.

I watched since I couldn't manage print to read—
the screen said sight would return to normal
as dilation time ran on its own slow speed
so watched visuals about conditions abnormal.

The screen said sight would return to normal,
computer users were especially at risk for dry eyes
so watched visuals about conditions abnormal
and noted white teeth on smiling young guys.

Computer users were especially at risk for dry eyes,
viewers were advised to use sunglasses outside,
and noted white teeth on smiling young guys:
was it possible there was some downside?

Viewers were advised to use sunglasses outside:
a line kept repeating We Accept Most Credit Cards:
was it possible there was some downside
memorizing many recommended safeguards.

A line kept repeating We Accept Most Credit Cards
waiting for the yearly eye exam to resume
memorizing many recommended safeguards:
visuals were on a screen in the waiting room.

A Beginning

Dawn, invading the room—a small bedroom that didn't yet reveal its corners—moved with the inexorable passage of time as it was in so many other rooms revealing subtleties when it was ready.

The room—an ordinary one in the Midwest was built with an eye for cost cutting and boasted a walk-in closet and large alcove between the window and the door filled with shelves. Vague forms hinted where the shelves were on the expanse of white wall as light advanced with its imperceptible speed.

The historian could have easily detected clues about the rise of the human species from the type of shelter and how adequately it advanced it since cave man days; the sociologist could have written much on the effect of living in such a house had for man as a social animal and the development of the family; an architect, the progress and popularity of low to the ground ranch homes in the United States no matter the region and for all incomes.

The ranch house is attributed to being American in origin—the one story floor plan with attached garage and shutters can be seen about anywhere. The landscape it was on did much to make it look different.

A Fun Jumble

E Pluribus Unum
and thereby hangs a tale.

Déjà vu
Devil to pay.

Ergo
Eureka!

Idioms, all idioms told by an idiot signifying
Tango, Tantalus, Tanzania.

Do I dare?
Earp, Wyatt
Ears, little pitchers.

You can't make an omelet without
breaking eggs.
Embryo
Embryology
Emerson, Ralph Waldo.

Not original?
Freely, Creeley, Dealey Do.
How does your garden grow?

Sing a song of pinched pennies
Pockets full of holes.

Jack and Jill went up the hill
To fetch a bale of fodder.

Are you pleading stop, stop?
The center cannot hold.

When Young

I thought when I was
older I'd have the
answers because questions
have answers.

By middle age insight
would come—
it was only logical.

But answers remain
shifting shadows.

Solar Eclipses

In the past, virgins were sacrificed to restore light—
after a few minutes the sun would reappear.
Sudden darkness created such widespread blight
in the past, virgins were sacrificed to restore light
as temperature dropped, strange twilight a dreaded sight,
unseen monsters devouring the sun spread great fear.
In the past, virgins were sacrificed to restore light—
after a few minutes the sun would reappear.

A Prufrock Measurement

I'm a connoisseur on how long drinks keep cold
and when they could drip down the sides:
an expert of how much ice drinks hold.
Wendy's red, white, gold, cups abide
as its redheaded girl takes one in stride.

McDonald's cups have the word thirst,
and a running Ronald tossing them in trash.
I'm not sure when golden arches appeared first
but they've surely multiplied, dispersed
everywhere I go with much bold abash.

Subway cups have arrows on their first and last
letters. The images of ice one can but presume
are designed to take one from despairing places
where women talk of Michelangelo with warm faces
and other topics one wisely dares not assume.

The Pleiades

There is a tale of seven sisters whose father held up the sky
pursued by Orion, carried to the heavens by Zeus.
Farming season began when their star cluster appeared high—
the position in the fall marked change in seafaring use.

Pursued by Orion, carried to the heavens by Zeus.
Among the first stars mentioned in ancient Chinese annals,
the position in the fall marked change in seafaring use—
with the Native American Kiowa taking similar channels.

Among the first stars mentioned in ancient Chinese annals
written around four thousand years ago—and as a myth
with the Native American Kiowa taking similar channels—
including the seven maidens' climb to Devil's Tower Monolith.

Written around four thousand years ago—and as a myth,
farming season began when their star cluster appeared high.
Including the seven maidens' climb to Devil's Tower Monolith
there is a tale of seven sisters whose father held up the sky.

Chameleon Light

What do we mean when we say the word, light? It all depends—
it is all up to how it's used; my dictionary has 53 definitions:
a popular word—noun, verb, adverb, adjective, it transcends.
What do we mean when we say the word, light? It all depends—
how our eyes detect is full of facts, amazing odds and ends
and what we choose to see comes down to individual positions.
What do we mean when we say the word, light? It all depends—
it is all up to how it's used; my dictionary has 53 definitions.

There are Many

kinds of microscopic plankton in the oceans—
but being so plentiful they're visible from space.

Named after a Greek word meaning, to wander,
they become rock when they die.

Arranging Spices on Your Shelf

By color—Basil, Chives, Parsley, Thyme:
Onion can be salt, granulated, minced.
An alphabetical list can be very long—big time
and I'm not sure many would be convinced.

Onion can be salt, granulated, minced:
Pepper: Cayenne, Seasoned, Black:
and I'm not sure many would be convinced
if rubs were included—there could be flack.

Pepper: Cayenne, Seasoned, Black;
by seed: Caraway, Celery, Dill:
if rubs were included there could be flack,
an arrangement questionable to fit the bill.

By seed: Caraway, Celery, Dill:
Leaves: Bay, Rosemary, Thyme
an arrangement questionable to fit the bill—
by now you've had enough of rhyme.

Leaves: Bay, Rosemary, Thyme
an alphabetical list can be very long—big time,
by now you've had enough of rhyme:
by color—Basil, Chives, Parsley, Thyme.

A Spider

was on the gas pump hanging by its line—
I knew it was a spider when it moved to the cement.
It was one of those black ones that jump,
a kind I never saw till moving to White Water.

When filling my tank I wondered if it were around
when gas was not yet oil before the sky was blue,
the smashing of asteroids and separating of continents,
the thunder of dinosaurs.

My tank full, I pushed a shopping list under it
and it went the other way; I moved the list and the
spider climbed by its line into a bag.

When home, I carried it to the woods where it caught
its line on waiting Queen Anne's Lace.

Color of Water

The color of water is said to be light blue
but has no color in small amounts.
Vapor is invisible, clouds gather new
then pile darkly as in a storm brew
turning rain and snow to an overhead stew
warned in daily weather accounts.
The color of water is said to be light blue
but has no color in small amounts.

On Hot Summer Days

the neighborhood kids would stop for me
on their way to go swimming in a lake
formed by glaciers ribbed on the bottom
with scalloped sand. It was shallow for a
long way before quickly becoming deep.

The brave thing was going underwater
with your eyes open to prove you could—
but what was better was watching the
bobbing heads of other kids above the lake—
and check where your clothes were just dots
on shore while listening to planes too far
away to see.

It's Immaterial

where to find material—
mud's often the most ethereal

Epilogue

A Green So Emerald

There is a green so emerald it hurts the eyes
that only comes with rains of early spring—
the color so brilliant it shouts, defies.
There is a green so emerald it hurts the eyes
that flourishes even under grayest skies
and confounds the ordinary that days bring.
There is a green so emerald it hurts the eyes
that only comes with rains of early spring.

Carol Smallwood's over five dozen books include *Women on Poetry: Writing, Revising, Publishing and Teaching,* on *Poets & Writers Magazine* list of Best Books for Writers. Recent anthologies include: *Writing After Retirement: Tips by Successful Retired Writers* (Rowman & Littlefield, 2014); *Bringing the Arts into the Library: An Outreach Handbook* (American Library Association, 2014); *Water, Earth, Air, Fire, and Picket Fences* (Lamar University Press, 2014), *Divining the Prime Meridian* (WordTech Editions, 2015). Her most recent literary collections are from Shanti Arts, 2017: *Interweavings: Creative Nonfiction, In Hubble's Shadow,* and *Library Partnerships with Writers and Poets: Case Studies (McFarland).* Carol has founded, supports humane societies. She's received multiple Pushcart Prize nominations and appears in *Who's Who in America; Who's Who in the World.*

www.ingramcontent.com/pod-product-compliance
Lightning Source LLC
Chambersburg PA
CBHW070549090426
42735CB00013B/3119